MUSINGS OF A MUSLIM CHAPLAIN

MUSINGS

of a

MUSLIM CHAPLAIN

Sondos Kholaki

Cover design: Tarek Kholaki

Editors: Baraa Kahf & Munira Lekovic Ezzeldine

ISBN: 1-6587-2650-2
ISBN 13: 978-1-6587-2650-4

None of us got this far in our lives and on our challenging journeys without a tribe of people — whether it's a tribe of 2 or 2,000 — who lovingly carried, uplifted, nourished, held, taught, pushed, and cautioned us. I hold deep gratitude and prayerful appreciation for all those who believe in me far more than I ever do/did.

هَذَا مِنْ فَضْلِ رَبِّيَ الْكَرِيْم

(Hatha min fadl Rabi al Kareem)
All of this is from the grace of God,
my Generous Nourisher and Sustainer

CONTENTS

Preface   ix

Foreword   xi

Introduction   xv

Chapter One: Chaplaincy   1

Chapter Two: Community   23

Chapter Three: Heart Work   35

Chapter Four: Returning   45

Chapter Five: God's Plan   53

Chapter Six: The Qur'an   61

Chapter Seven: Prayer and Worship   67

Chapter Eight: Children   77

About the Author   85

PREFACE

This book is a curated selection of daily journal entries and musings of Sondos Kholaki, a hospital chaplain, which she posted on social media between 2016 and 2019. Entries have been minimally edited to add translations and provide context where appropriate. Names and identifying details have been removed to protect the privacy of individuals.

FOREWORD

In the Name of God, the Most Merciful and
Compassionate

When one speaks of grief, it is often from the
vantage point of either the one in such a state, or the
one theorizing on the various ways to contend with it.
The musings contained within this book do neither.
Instead, Sondos Kholaki has presented us with a
volume of insightful and authentic musings of a servant
of the human spirit – the most fragile thing in the
universe, yet also the most powerful. Loss and suffering
offer insights into this apparent paradox in a manner
like no other aspect of the human condition. It would
be remiss, then, to speak of loss and grief without also
mentioning resolve, forbearance, and beauty. Chaplain
Sondos conveys these elements via her interactions with
those experiencing grief in her hospital setting. Her
insights are imbued with her religious commitment, in a
manner that endears, regardless of one's own religious
convictions. This, in essence, is the true promise of
religious faith – its ability, at its best, to transcend and
affect by appealing to the best of our shared humanity.

At its worst, it becomes a blunt instrument to impugn and imperil those who do not conform to reductionist concepts of piety.

As Chaplain Sondos shares her thoughts with her readership, she also shares aspects of the "inner life." According to Islamic teachings, this inner life forms the arena of true connection to God. One's external actions are ultimately the result of one's inner workings and thought processes. By extension, suffering, and concomitant manifestations of grief, can take an individual down a number of pathways. For the spiritually uncultivated, emotional trauma commensurate with great loss often leads to displacement of the psychological wounds via the inflicting of similar harms upon others, and often oneself. An argument can be made that the inability of the traumatized to process their trauma is the root cause for much of the suffering and harm human beings inflict upon one another. This pervasive cycle of grief driven toxicity can only be broken by healing. Healing can only occur via healers – those who have dedicated their existence to help others help themselves.

Chaplain Sondos invites us into the world of the healer. Her insights curated from her own experiences via her commitment to God and service to humanity offer the reader a glimpse into some of the most important human work occurring today. She accords the reader a great honor and privilege, one that should not be taken for granted. I pray that it serves as guidance and inspiration for all healers, of all religious traditions and ideological affiliations, for though the individual hearts are many, their source of light remains One.

Walead Mohammed Mosaad
Director of Muslim Student Life
Lehigh University
Bethlehem, Pennsylvania

INTRODUCTION

Suffering – as a concept and a reality – manifests itself intensely in the hospital setting. As a chaplain, I witness the various forms of suffering on a daily basis when visiting patients, family, and staff with myriad physical, emotional, mental, and spiritual wounds. Patients may writhe in their cramped bed from the pain, others cry out for absent loved ones, and yet others escape inward with no reaction to outside stimuli. The patients, families, and staff for whom chaplains seek to provide spiritual care experience the impact of suffering on multiple, existential dimensions at once. Just as suffering manifests itself in various forms, understanding and making meaning out of suffering remains just as varied, particularly within a religious context. As a chaplain, I aim to join the patient in making meaning of pain and suffering by exploring how this coincides with their understanding of the Divine.

Suffering and loss are embedded into the fabric of our lives. People of faith may anticipate life's trials to confront them, no less with particular acuity in light of the Qur'an stating, "Do people think that they will be left to say, 'We believe' and they will not be tried?" (29:2). Yet, somehow, even as we may intuit that and understand the need to have our hearts and spirits crushed under the weight of life's greatest tests – be they upon our physical health or a loved one's; loss of emotional or mental balance; decreases to our material means; or a crisis impacting our very sense of meaning – few people, "faithful" or otherwise, may be prepared to withstand even a single of these factors going into decline, let alone a combination of several of them. Suffering is a distinctive journey and discovery for each individual. In other words, pain – an experience felt by everybody at some capacity at some point in their lives – serves as the impetus for an inward search and gradual discernment of the Divine.

The Islamic tradition is replete with instances of God informing us of His Divine Presence with the sick, the broken hearted, and the oppressed. It is in suffering that we call out to God from the depths of the whale

(Qur'an 21:87), or from the ship tossed at sea (17:67), or from a consuming illness (21:83). In pain, at its most intense, we find ourselves folded over, in need, surrendered, and humbled, just as Mary finds herself when commanded by God to "prostrate and bow with those who bow [in prayer]" (3:43).

When we surrender to the pain and lean into it – not avoid it nor distract from it – we can open ourselves to the presence of God. Otherwise, we remain our own barrier between the Divine and ourselves. Nothing ever veils God from the servant, but in situations of dire extremity, God's intense proximity is not measured in distance but in His Merciful relenting to the servant's plea, being swift in response. We can imagine so many scenarios where one is oppressed or constricted by their circumstances, and in their desperation, they come to realize that God alone is their refuge to a way forward. Sincere seekers of God understand the undeniable link between God's self-asserted presence with those experiencing the ultimate rawness of pain such that God reveals Himself to the one calling out for Him when all the rest of His creation fail to meet one's needs. At some point in the tribulation, to recognize that God is the only One who understands fully the complexities of the situation at hand, the only One who hears the spoken and unspoken cries of the heart, the only One who knows with certainty the outcome ahead, the only One who – in His limitless Gentleness and Mercy – can offer a blanket of peace and tranquility amid the pain, and the only One who can do all of this without so much a word uttered from the lips of the oppressed, is to arrive at a station so humbled that one surrenders oneself completely to Him.

In serving as a chaplain, in learning to sit in the pain instead of running away from it, I began to acknowledge the reality that to be human is to suffer. I began to recognize that we are all in this pain together, all of us carrying a burden and struggling to "make it" on our individual journeys. When I could acknowledge this, I began to operate out of humility and hospitality unlike any other time of my life thus far. As chaplains, we take in wandering travelers looking for a moment of rest and encouragement to be able to return to their journey. We may not succeed in helping them find their destination, but at least we may offer a moment of relief for the traveler to remove their heavy burden to rest before hoisting it back up and continuing on. This is how we create community – when we can be vulnerable with one another, when we can see each other as equals in our struggles, that is when we can connect on a deeper level. Through the unusual, highly unexpected and, at times, bewildering confluence of people and circumstances in which God has placed me, as part of my necessary spiritual discipline, written in pre-eternity but lived and delighted and wept over in the here and now, suffering became the doorway to my *hudhur* (full presence) in the moment. Remember a time when you felt incredible physical pain; in that state, one finds it difficult to focus on anything but the present moment, from one breath to the next. Past and future dissolve because the energy needed to summon or create those realities prove too much to bear alongside the pain. Can we train ourselves to really sit into the suffering, not to gulp it down or throw it out, but to wade in the experience, to host this emotional guest of the moment and eventually ask, what is this pain teaching me?

I came to the Clinical Pastoral Education (CPE) program at the hospital as the only Muslim, largely inexperienced in life's greatest trials and tribulations, and a "novice" in matters relating to critical illness or death. I saw my first dead body in the Emergency Department, after the patient dropped to the pavement in the middle of his morning jog and never awoke. I remember that he still had on his sneakers when the doctor called the time of death, his frantic wife at the bedside begging her husband to "wake up." Through my internship, my yearlong residency, and my current position as staff, I bore witness to many, many more instances of death, of hearts breaking, of anger at God, of human beings disintegrating into themselves following unbearable news. My most important – though, not only – task in those moments was to witness people's agonizing pain. Early on in my internship, I could not bear this task and, instead, found any excuse to run out of the room, whether it was to fetch someone water or a blanket or a nurse. Slowly, gradually, with better training and more experience, I learned to sit still and hold space for the pain to unfold. This sitting still, this witnessing, proved transformative in mysterious ways.

Once, I sat with a patient's family member whose own personal burdens drove them to confide in me in a hallway for over an hour. In previous days, this family member had lashed out verbally at the staff and displayed an overall volatile state. Following our hallway conversation, I walked this individual back to the patient's room where other relatives stared at their loved one in surprise. "Your face … it looks different; more peaceful," one of them noted about the individual, who smiled softly and replied, "That's because I *feel* more peaceful." I was amazed. In the hour of our conversation, I spoke for only a handful of minutes, and for the rest of the time, I listened actively with full presence, witnessing the pain and struggle of this individual's grief. It makes me wonder why we humans have such an innate need to witness and be witnessed, and how that is foundational to relationship building and connection. A chaplain colleague once shared with me that our faith's creed, as the basis for a human's most primary relationship, begins with affirmation through witnessing, such that perhaps every other significant human relationship thereafter is the servant's best attempt to approximate, recreate, and preserve the Primary relationship upon which all contentment and peace is grounded.

I consider the fruits born of my experience in hospital chaplaincy in the last three years and how it intertwines with a rebirth of my spiritual life. Chaplaincy – its theory and practice – has gifted me back my connection to God in a way that years of sermons, classes, lectures, books, and research could have never accomplished. Throughout my residency, I returned to my books to study carefully the life of the Prophet Muhammad ﷺ (peace be upon him). In doing so, I realized the gaps in how I teach and was taught the religion of Islam; that is, often through rituals and rules without first engaging the heart. Spiritual and prophetic care is heart-centered, not head-centered. It is not in *spite* of our tradition that we will grow but in *reviving* our tradition, in the way of our beloved Prophet ﷺ, that our spiritual connection will flourish and thrive and survive.

Our beloved ﷺ spent the majority of his time among the needy, and I wonder now if the "needy" is not limited to monetary means. In our day and age, perhaps those who are "needy" are also those who are spiritually broken. It is from the life and example of the beloved Prophet ﷺ that I learn how to honor every human soul by listening attentively and being present to them; how to respond to grieving families in bereavement; how to meet people where they are in their spiritual journey; how to empower individuals to advocate for themselves; how to employ reflective questioning to help others find answers to burning questions; how to display emotion vulnerably and authentically such that connections can endure; and more. The example of the Prophet Muhammad ﷺ informs my ministry and service to others. Addressing the Prophet ﷺ directly, God states in the Qur'an, "We have not sent you except as a mercy to the worlds" (21:107). The implications of this teaching are far and wide. Muslim scholarship throughout the ages establishes this verse as illuminating the central ethos of Islamic life: to emulate the prophetic call of becoming an embodiment and means by which to extend love towards neighbor and humanity, and mercy towards all creation. No person, and, in fact, no creature should be spared the fullest offering of mercy and compassion that we can summon.

In CPE, I learned that every person is a "living human document" in that we are constantly writing and rewriting our narratives, and these narratives deserve careful study and analysis as any sacred scripture or scholarly text. Our Prophet ﷺ understood that people move and deepen and grow in delicate, layered stages of faith. The prophetic way of seeing people, then, is to have a good opinion of others and see their potential for growth, and, by extension, to have a good opinion of God. The Prophet ﷺ had this wisdom with people; he ﷺ was tuned into their humanity, their dignity, and their worth in the eyes of God. During my time at the hospital, and the more journeys I am honored to witness, the more I understand just how people are formed by and react from their circumstances and experiences, which fortifies my belief that God holds each of us accountable differently.

If we consider our own trajectories, where we were spiritually ten years ago, we can begin to appreciate all the ways in which we have grown. Can we remember the people who were patient with us during our growth in those ten years, who saw potential in us and told us that we were still developing and that they would journey alongside us through it all? Who are those people for you? When we train ourselves to see the good and potential in everybody, we cultivate sincere love in our hearts for them. Through this loving accompaniment, we may extend to another an opportunity to heal by meeting them where they are, while empowering and affirming them. A seasoned chaplain mentor once told me, "If you listen to somebody long enough, they'll tell you what's weighing on them. If you listen a little longer, they'll tell you how to solve it."

Sitting at another vista of personal, spiritual, and emotional growth and tension, I no longer presume to believe there is a single formula – verbal or gestural – that will soften the shock and incomprehension brought on by the assaults upon the frail, so tender human spirit. But there are ways forward. Because what we can affirm and what we can seek to explore in our lives are the pathways towards a Divinely-prescribed (and described) easing and lightening found within the experience of suffering and great trials. The Qur'an says in the chapter titled "Expansion," "Indeed, with the difficulty there is an ease; indeed, with the difficulty there is an ease" (94:5-6). It appears quite significant that the Qur'an leaves ambiguous what this vital element of ease amid difficulty may comprise. But we understand this ease to be enfolded, enigmatically, into the journey itself. Moreover, this is one of only two verses in the Qur'an that repeat one another in precise wording, in consecutive form. Perhaps God wants us to embrace this maxim, even while leaving us to discover, and in the fullness of time, thrive in its reality – the potential for expansion amid constriction.

It may take me many more years in chaplaincy to understand what such ease amid difficulty looks or feels like, or how it can be summoned. Or, it may be understood in a mere instant. God alone discloses such knowledge. For now, I hold true to the belief that as we deepen our intention and practice of joining with one another at our most vulnerable, so too, we might find the Divine Mercy permeating our life's path. This meaning is alluded to in the teaching of the Prophet Muhammad ﷺ when he said, "The beloved servant of God will find God's assistance ever at hand as long as they are in the assistance of their fellow human being." In hindsight, I am acquiring an awareness that *ishq* (love) can be a life-altering reality that reshapes and repurposes the soul to a higher disposition of spiritual and emotional character, so that one becomes love, personified. Whatever emotions surface for us in the reading of these encounters, I hope we will permit ourselves to pause and attempt to identify and wade in the feeling(s) to open up to our authentic selves.

CHAPTER ONE

CHAPLAINCY

September 6, 2016

This morning, our internship orientation was held in the hospital chapel. As we walked in, I knew I had been in that space before. I had a flashback of being at that exact chapel several years ago while visiting a sick friend. I remembered admiring the prayer space and studying the telephone that connects to a chaplain.

Something sparked inside me that day, and I recall thinking, "I'd love to be the chaplain who hurting people would call on that phone."

Fast forward many years later, and God brings me back full circle to the exact same chapel at the same hospital branch for my chaplaincy internship orientation. Praise God.

***

December 28, 2016

As a hospital chaplain, I learned that my every day is somebody else's worst day.

***

March 1, 2017

A "good" chaplain visit involves asking the right questions, not having the right answers.

***

June 21, 2017

Coming into CPE (Clinical Pastoral Education) last September, I learned an important lesson: as a chaplain, I am not there to fix it. Regretfully, most of my first visits were spent fetching water and coffee, bringing blankets, calling nurses, reading Scripture, and avoiding uncomfortable silences at all costs. Even now, I notice that when I am anxious, I resort back to these "fixing" norms and must pause and assess the source of my discomfort.

As I learned to lean into the discomfort and more about the art of spiritual care, I had to train myself in the "being" instead of "doing" and found it to make all the difference in a visit. It took many hours of education and clinical experiences to train myself in this new awareness, in self-restraint, and in holding myself back from giving advice and offering solutions. One way I trained myself was by practicing on my children. Whenever they came to me with a complaint or concern, I asked them, "Are you telling me this because you're looking for advice or for empathy?" More times than not, the answer was "empathy."

The pastoral style of the Prophet Muhammad ﷺ (peace be upon him) was in being, not doing; he would absorb himself completely in the narrative of the other, even turning his entire body toward the person speaking. According to many narrators, this attention from the Prophet ﷺ was so pronounced, it made the individual feel like they were the most important person to him. For many of us, we have lost this practice of "being" with one another, and we need to retrain

3

ourselves to embody it even though this level of active listening requires much focus.

This renunciation of doing, or inhabiting the role of "the fixer," is one of the most challenging aspects of hospital chaplaincy for me. I struggle with needing tangible evidence to assure that I did "well" or whether I helped in any way, and most of the time, I must leave an encounter having to accept that there may be no closure or continuation of the dialogue after the patient's discharge home.

***

July 7, 2017

> … I soon began to trust the process of stepping into [people's] narrative worlds and following their lead in ways similar to how I followed the storyline of a novel. I soon discovered that pastoral care was not just a matter of listening to these unfolding stories. It was also about creating meaning.
> —*The Practice of Pastoral Care*

Until I read this excerpt from a spiritual care book, I never thought about how my B.A. in Literature and my long-time love for reading and writing connected to chaplaincy. These lines struck me so much so that I put down the book and just marveled at God's intricate planning. *SubhanAllah* (glory to God) how all the threads tie up along the journey!

***

July 24, 2017

As I take some time to reflect on my brother's wedding this past weekend, I'm struck by the parallels between marriage and chaplaincy. Both require trust in God for guidance, a growing skill in communication, and a foundation in love and service. Both are sacred spaces cultivated by two people with a deep desire for connection. Both are successful when God is prioritized.

May God bless and protect the newlyweds and grant them a lifetime of happiness together *inshaAllah* (God willing). *Ameen.*

***

July 28, 2017

Serving as a Muslim chaplain in the hospital is challenging. Not only do I get puzzled looks from non-Muslim patients when I introduce myself as the chaplain, I get even more puzzled looks from the Muslim patients! They don't know what to make of me.

What exactly do I do? Am I a rogue female *Imam* (religious leader)? Am I a type of nurse? Am I a volunteer from the *masjid* (mosque)? Sometimes I explain that I'm there for emotional and spiritual support, but that doesn't resonate either.

I have yet to figure out how to accurately translate my title so that the Muslim community can take advantage of much needed pastoral care services available to them at the hospital. How can I better educate my community in this regard?

***

September 11, 2017

I was reminded today that one of the major learning curves of hospital chaplaincy is leaning into the discomfort.

This reminder came in handy when I visited a patient in severe withdrawal from alcohol poisoning. He was shaking violently and sweating. His breath smelled sour and putrid, and he had dry, cracked lips. He struggled to speak clearly, so I had to literally lean in to hear him every time he opened his mouth. I wanted to gag. I wanted to run out. I wanted to make any excuse to leave. But I leaned in. And when I did, I heard him say, "Thank you for staying with me. Do you have to leave soon? Please stay," as he gripped my hand from his bed restraints. He was alone and scared, so I stayed. I can still smell his sour breath, but I know his words will remain with me far longer.

***

September 26, 2017

Today, I visited with a patient who has been hospitalized for a week. She is a mom of young kids and was eager to resume their routine. When I asked her what she was looking forward to the most upon getting home, she closed her eyes and said in a wistful voice, "a shower." She repeated it a few more times, her eyes still closed. She added, "And then, sleeping in my bed. Sleeping till I wake up on my own, not because someone is knocking at the door or drawing blood or taking my vitals."

It struck me that I do these two tasks every day, most of the time without a second thought. It really is about the "little" things, isn't it, and more about what they symbolize in our life.

***

November 3, 2017

I visited with two suicidal patients this week. Both are from completely different backgrounds, religions, and personal situations. However, both used the same exact word to describe their current emotion: empty. One said she feels like a room in a house that has just been stripped of its long-time furniture. As I sit into that image, I feel an overwhelming loneliness and loss.

May God ease the pain of those who feel this incredible burden of emptiness. May God send them peace and comfort.

***

November 29, 2017

The combination of prayer and chaplaincy has been a fascinating experience for me. To be designated as the Prayer Person and to be asked to pray aloud for somebody in deep distress whose hope lies in the power of your words and your connection and "role," who grabs on to your hand so tightly as though to stay afloat, it's both extraordinarily humbling and terrifying. Praying for your own needs is one thing; coming up with the words, feelings, and needs of a stranger is another. May God accept from us all.

***

February 1, 2018

Recently, I was asked to give a five minute talk summarizing Islamic Pastoral (or Spiritual) Care and how/when it differs from other "flavors" of pastoral care. After consulting several sources, I came up with these five points that I hope will be useful for others:

1. Islamic Pastoral Care is rooted in the Qur'an and life/example of Prophet Muhammad ﷺ. The Qur'an is emotionally and spiritually central to every Muslim's life; verses are often used for healing, prayer, and guidance. The life of the Prophet ﷺ is our model and inspiration for pastoral care.

2. Islamic Pastoral Care emphasizes hospitality. This means creating a welcoming environment using presence, active listening, compassion, and connection (regardless of the careseeker's faith background). We are taught the particulars of this hospitality by the example of the Prophet ﷺ.

3. Islamic Pastoral Care incorporates the Islamic legal tradition and ritual when applicable. The legal tradition manifests itself in the hospital context in end of life decisions, biomedical ethics, and other directive education situations. By ritual, I mean facilitating prayer, reciting Qur'an, etc.

4. Islamic Pastoral Care aims to bring hope, comfort, and peace to the careseeker, but also, it is to find meaning and purpose in the suffering based on our tradition/theology.

5. Islamic Pastoral Care is representative of the larger Muslim community, or *ummah*. The caregiver is the connection to and representative of all the resources offered by our community. This means if the caregiver cannot provide a service, he/she can connect to somebody in the immediate community who can.

***

March 2, 2018

In studying chaplaincy, I learned that the word "chaplain" evolved from the Latin word, "cappa," or cloak. I thought of all that a cloak symbolizes: warmth, protection, security, and concealment, and how all those qualities overlap with what a chaplain aims to provide for the careseeker.

And then I was struck by the story of Khadija (God be pleased with her), when she covered the Prophet ﷺ with a cloak after he returned from his retreat terrified and confused. In that moment of his distress, Khadija comforted and supported him. She "chaplained" him, the one from whose perfect example our pastoral care strives to emulate. Now I'll read *Surat Al Muzzamil* (Qur'an Chapter 73) in a whole new light!

***

May 1, 2018

Sometimes, it's not helpful to introduce yourself as a chaplain to the family of a sick elderly patient in the ER. Relearned this lesson today.

***

May 17, 2018

No two of us have identical difficulties,
nor should we be expected to work out
identical solutions.
—William James

This is why chaplains explore rather than explain.

***

July 8, 2018

Speak a good word or remain silent.
—Prophet Muhammad ﷺ

In my time at the hospital, I have served a few patients who lost their ability to speak, either due to illness or trauma. The experience often leaves me reflecting on the power of speech, specifically of the weight of words. Imagine being given a handful of words with which to tell your story; which parts would you tell? What details would you include or leave out?

With limited conversation, I as chaplain focus on what really needs to be asked, and they as patient create other ways to communicate, sometimes by phone text, drawings, or pen and paper. Small talk is usually brief. Useless speech is nonexistent. Words become deliberate, pointed, emphasized, honed, precious. Eyes and hands become important tools for communication. A smile goes a long, long way.

***

August 15, 2018

At the intersection of joy and grief:

As I turned the corner headed for a patient's room, I recognized a familiar face — a woman whose loved one I had just visited the day before. This woman was crying and came over for a hug. As I wrapped my arms around her, I looked up and saw two more familiar faces right behind her — an older couple, beaming at me. I recognized the wife from a couple weeks ago as she was a patient herself in bad shape. Her husband was ever

12

present by her side and always asked for prayers from me when I checked in with them on my floor.

Now, there she was, healthy and happy. As they greeted me, I remembered I was wrapped in a hug by a woman whose loved one was not doing so well. I was caught in that moment between sharing in the couple's joy and grieving with the woman. It felt confusing, overwhelming. I wasn't sure if it was tactful of me to even acknowledge the joy, but how could I not? As the woman pulled back from the hug, she stood next to the couple. Turns out they were friends; the healed wife was there with her husband to support this woman through her loved one's hospitalization.

We were all connected in that moment, but in very different ways.

***

September 17, 2018

I was walking down the unit hallway when I heard yelling from a patient's room. I turned to look at a nearby nurse quizzically, to which she shrugged and said, "Neurological. Maybe Tourette's." Thinking to myself, "Well, not much I can do there," I turned around and continued down the hall. The nurse called out, "Hey, you're walking the wrong way." Ouch.

Half embarrassed, half challenged, I went into the patient's room with some trepidation. The hour long visit turned out to be one of the most affirming experiences of my chaplaincy career.

Chase/follow the pain instead of walking away from it.

***

October 6, 2018

Once I visited with a younger patient who spent almost two weeks undergoing surgeries for ongoing pain. I asked her what the most challenging part of her journey was, and her answer surprised me. She replied without hesitation, "That nobody believed me."

Prior to being admitted, she had spent six months telling her family, doctors, emergency departments, friends, etc. that something wasn't right with her body, and everybody wrote her off as dramatic or whiny. All she wanted was somebody to see, hear, and affirm her pain as her truth.

***

October 30, 2018

When do I see a chaplain?

#1 Spiritual crisis: One who suffers from spiritual imbalance following a significant event that leaves one questioning prior spiritual truths.

Following said event, one undergoes a jarring and scary process of discerning which spiritual truths remain, which need adjustment, and which may need discarding.

One may be experiencing a transition from one level of faith to another. Spiritual accompanying by a qualified chaplain may help in the transition.

***

October 31, 2018

When do I see a chaplain?

#2 Broken connection: When one experiences a heightened state of fear, anxiousness, apprehension, or hopelessness that impedes his/her ability to connect to the Holy.

A qualified chaplain may help facilitate a deeper exploration of the emotions blocking an authentic connection and/or search out alternative ways of connection.

***

November 1, 2018

When do I see a chaplain?

#3 When one requires assistance in securing resources – human or otherwise – from his/her faith community, as well as assistance in facilitation of religious ritual at work, school, or any location that requires one's extended presence.

A qualified chaplain serves as a facilitator and advocate for the careseeker's spiritual and religious needs.

***

November 2, 2018

When do I see a chaplain?

#4 One may be seeking guidance related to ethical or spiritual matters such as purpose and meaning, suffering and pain, hopes and fears, value and worth. A qualified chaplain provides a confidential, open, and

16

non-judgmental space for reflection to assist the individual in moving forward.

***

November 5, 2018

When do I see a chaplain?

#5 Community and connection: When one has been or is in the process of becoming disenchanted with his/her faith community but retains a longing for spiritual fellowship and revival.

A qualified chaplain may support this individual in defining and finding a community that complements one's preference for spiritual nourishment. At a minimum, a qualified chaplain sustains a crucial link to one's faith community by providing an opportunity for deep and intentional connection through hospitable listening, affirmation, and accompaniment.

***

December 15, 2018

"Remember that *everyone* is hurting"

One of the biggest lessons I've learned from chaplaincy. Let's revive the *sunnah* (prophetic teachings) of compassion, dear friends. We need each other in our most authentic state.

***

December 27, 2018

Picking up some pre op prayer orders this week, and I realized that it's not a part of the job that I especially enjoy. I always psyche myself out trying to say the "right" prayer for the patient, some words to bring comfort and peace and ease anxiousness. This morning as I did rounds, I remembered a lesson from my days at the Islamic Center — people remember how you made them feel, not what you said.

So, as I walk into my next visit, I hope to approach the meeting with these questions: Did my presence communicate peace and tranquility? Did I impart a sense of hope in a good outcome? Did I make him or her feel seen and appreciated and joined?

Allah help us reach the sacred meanings beyond the recited words, always. *Ameen.*

***

April 1, 2019

Our job as a presence in another's spiritual journey is not to push them but to cushion them through their growth. #revivingthesunnahofcompassion

May 23, 2019

I can attest to the humbling transformation of self that comes by way of caring for the most vulnerable and raw. There's a sacred secret in compassion and service to others that we must reclaim, as best exemplified by the beloved Prophet ﷺ.

***

June 22, 2019

Religion is a complex phenomenon.

I had two back to back visits. The first requested prayers and a blessing from a specific tradition for a patient at the end of life. The prayers and a blessing brought the family much comfort and relief at bedside.

Immediately afterward, I visited with a patient who was raised in the same tradition as the first patient but who felt disassociated from that community due to perceived hypocrisy and atrocities committed by people. That patient felt no comfort, no relief from that tradition but rather had to start from scratch to reconstruct her spiritual truths.

What nourishes and sustains us may not translate in similar ways for another. Thankfully, God is Nuanced and Merciful to understand our individual circumstances and struggles. Let's commit to extending some of this nuance and mercy to one another.

***

October 9, 2019

I met with a patient who carries a very heavy burden. After she shared her story with me, she asked, "Is this going to ruin your entire afternoon and evening? Are you going to be depressed by what I shared?" I assured her that our training prepares us well for this and affirmed her beautiful heart for worrying about me amid her myriad struggles.

Two hours later, I wonder if what she was really asking was, "Will you remember me after you leave the hospital and return to your home life? Did I make any impact upon you worth remembering?"

She absolutely did. Wish I could tell her so.

***

November 28, 2019

My professional (chaplaincy) and personal (in life) guidepost based on a central maxim in Islam:

"Do no harm."

***

CHAPTER TWO

COMMUNITY

October 26, 2016

This morning, chaplain interns discussed racism and how it manifests itself as racial superiority (e.g., my color is better than yours). From there, we delved into spiritual superiority (e.g., my religion/God/faith is better than yours). I began to wonder how many other ways we humans internalize and propagate prejudice in our daily lives. May God grant us this self-awareness as we journey in our constant struggle for self-improvement. *Ameen.*

***

November 2, 2016

Only in America does a Muslim chaplain at a Presbyterian hospital minister to a non-denominational Christian who is actually a "secret" Catholic. This experience I had yesterday made me pause and reflect on religious labels and our insistence on division. The more time I spend at the hospital, the more I discover God.

***

November 14, 2016

Today, I went to work at the hospital and shared with a fellow chaplain coworker that I was sad to miss my son's award ceremony this morning due to a speaking engagement. It would be the first ceremony I miss since he started school. She immediately jumped up and asked if she could go in my place.

She is a familiar face to my kids, who visit my office often. She treats them to chips and candy and a lot of hugs. So she got permission from our lead chaplain, drove to his school, took pictures and eighteen video clips, and cheered her heart out for him. His big smile in each of her pictures made my heart melt as I sat many miles away.

This chaplain coworker does not share my faith nor my political views. And she deeply loves me and my family and has said on many occasions that she would never let anybody touch my family.

This is my America, where radically different political and religious individuals can love and respect each other and become like family, where we protect one another's rights and dignity. It's the gray area we can start exploring together.

***

December 16, 2016

Ministering to a patient's wife this morning, and the following ensued:

Wife: You're Muslim, right?
Me: Yes.
Wife: I just want you to know that I have no hate in my heart toward you.

Sad that we have to make that distinction nowadays.

***

February 6, 2017

Gone is the era of "not my problem;" today, we will ask, "Why do you fear?"

We can no longer afford to say, "I don't understand;" today, we will seek to walk in another's shoes.

Differences should be opportunities to explore, not exclude.

***

February 24, 2017

Just came out of a visit with a Christian patient who burst into tears when I confirmed that I was a Muslim. She said, "I'm so happy. I have always wanted to meet a Muslim."

God is Awesome.

***

April 11, 2017

I was just visiting with a young patient who was hospitalized for overdosing. During the visit, she showed me an encouraging note written by a nurse on her hospital room whiteboard, and I asked her what she feels when she sees that message. "Love," she said softly with tears flooding her eyes.

It struck me that, as humans, we all look for those road signs that reassure us that we are loved. Show some love to another human today. God knows we could use it.

***

June 2, 2017

This morning, a Catholic patient told me that when he sees Muslim women, he surveys the crowd for troublemakers, at the ready to jump to the women's defense should anybody bother them. It felt good – as a Muslim covered woman – to know people like that are out there watching my back.

***

November 14, 2017

Chaplain colleague, today: "Please don't take this in the wrong way, but you're the most normal Muslim I've ever met."

Folks, we've got some work to do if he thinks I'm the normal one.

***

November 25, 2017

Relationships are like stocks; invest wisely and trust your instinct.

***

April 5, 2018

I know Muslims hold different opinions on *zabiha* (humanely slaughtered) meat, but I can appreciate that in a country where Muslims are the minority, purposefully choosing to eat at good Muslim-run establishments benefits our people. It reminds me of Malcolm X's encouragement to the black community to buy from African-American businesses as a form of empowerment and uplift. There's a wisdom to prioritizing *zabiha* (regardless of one's personal opinion) I never realized before, *subhanAllah*.

***

April 18, 2018

Last Ramadan, I visited an elderly Muslim man in the hospital. Because of his age and deteriorating health, he was not obligated to fast. He spent the entire visit complaining sadly to me that he wanted to fast but his family wasn't allowing him to do so. After trying unsuccessfully to convince him of the *rukhsa* (alleviation) of not fasting, I realized that perhaps what he was missing was what all of us miss when we don't fast in Ramadan for one reason or another: community, fellowship, a sense that we are a part of something much larger than anything else. He felt disconnected from the outside world during a special time.

This Ramadan, I want to bring some of that community and connection to the Muslim patients by way of a Ramadan box, an idea I heard from a fellow chaplain friend. My crowdsourcing question is, apart from food items, what can I put in these small boxes to communicate love, care, and community? A local school has already volunteered to have these boxes decorated by students, but I'd like some (affordable) ideas on what to put inside.

***

May 8, 2018

What a gift, as a caregiver/care provider, to need help from your fellow career community members: a surgeon needing surgery, a nurse becoming bedridden, a therapist dealing with family issues, a teacher going back to school, a lawyer needing expert counsel, and, of course, a chaplain struggling to answer deeper spiritual questions. It gives one a sense of the immediacy, urgency, hunger, and helplessness that comes with the incredibly humbling feeling of "not-knowing" the outcome and being at the mercy of another's skill, schedule, and opinion.

***

July 22, 2018

On this sticky hot afternoon, I found a dead rat in my garage. Temporarily without my brave husband, I texted my neighbors for help. They came with a shovel, a bag, Lysol spray, some good humor, and moral support. I already love my neighbors, but knowing they would go to lengths like bagging up a dead rat for me gives me all the feels.

In death, we often find community. Sometimes it takes even a little bit of darkness to draw attention to the light.

***

November 16, 2018

The Majlis (a spiritual and educational space in Southern California) is near and dear to my heart. As I was sitting among fellow beloved friends in The Majlis's "Believing Together" program last night, I marveled at the uniqueness of this project. It is the only space where I am fed and nourished, physically and spiritually; where I can have meaningful "small talk" with a Syrian grandmother, a young child, peers my age and 10 years younger and 10 years older; where the group engages in interactive worship and deep, reflective listening; where we have hours to enjoy spending time with our teachers; where people ask, "How are you?" and stop to hear your answer; where community becomes family ... really, truly family.

In all my life, I have never had the privilege to occupy such a space. Thursday nights have become sacred nights for our family, and I pray that with more resources deservedly funneled into The Majlis and its founders, the every-other-Thursday gatherings can become not just weekly, but every-other-day.

***

March 26, 2019

If you could only sense how important
you are to the lives of every person you
meet; how important you can be to the
people you never even dream of. There
is something of yourself that you leave
at every meeting with another person.
—Fred Rogers

This idea of leaving something with every person you meet is such a heavy *amana* (responsibility). We each have the potential to heal or harm in every interaction.

Allah help us to always be a means of healing and never of harm. *Ameen.*

***

May 9, 2019

A few Sundays ago, I was feeling depleted and exhausted after a long weekend of commitments. I debated whether to continue on to The Majlis evening program or go straight home, but my son was at the program already. I remember dragging myself up the stairs only to perk up slightly at the scent of sweet burning *oud* (incense). Making my way through the door, I was greeted with warm *salams* (greetings of peace) and, of course, an invitation to tea or coffee.

Seeing something in my eyes, the volunteer said, "I have something special for you. Wait a second." He proceeded to pull out a small jar of beautifully colorful herbs and took several minutes to steep it just right. When he handed it to me with such care and attention, I couldn't help but cry from relief. Somebody saw me, really saw me. And cared.

This is my experience at The Majlis, every week. And when I'm not exhausted, I try to be that person who's on the lookout for the weary who come through our doors. ***

May 19, 2019

I sat with an elderly patient who was born and raised in a region fraught with war and divisiveness. While we didn't see eye to eye on everything, her message was worth reflecting upon. Without more than a ten second pause after I asked her what she would advise the next generation of that region, she replied:

"One, do agriculture together. Two, educate children together. Three, practice medicine together."

In that, I heard: Plant seeds. Plant seeds. Heal and serve.

***

October 4, 2019

Today was my last day of intensives (on-campus portion of the semester) at Bayan Claremont.

Since today is Friday/*Jum'uah*, our daily homemade lunch was to be catered later in the afternoon, which meant that I'd miss it as I typically drive straight to work after class. Concerned about my nourishment, a Bayan staff member asked me no less than five times on different occasions if he could get me lunch from across the street. "You're the only one not staying, and I can't let you leave without lunch," he said. Not wanting to inconvenience him, I tried to decline. Finally, upon his sweet insistence and care, I gratefully acquiesced. He returned an hour later with a carefully wrapped, healthy lunch.

To me, this is the epitome of Bayan's ethos. They're not only facilitating for the most extraordinary faculty to train students to be the most effective servant-leaders, those running Bayan are modeling servant-leadership in the most loving, humble, and meaningful ways. I learned more from watching those around me, be it staff, faculty, or students, than I did in the (many, many, many) texts.

I started the Master of Divinity program in Fall 2015, and now, four years later, I'm counting down to the semester's end in December. I'll miss my Bayan family like crazy, but know I'll be praying for you all forever *inshaAllah*.

***

CHAPTER THREE

HEART WORK

May 11, 2016

Responding with love and mercy is not a sign of weakness.

***

July 16, 2016

Sometimes the person who needs a hug the most is the one who shows it the least.

***

January 3, 2017

If we don't risk, we don't fail. If we don't fail, we cultivate a dangerous sense of security.

My learning theme this season: Risk. Fail. Be humbled. Turn to God. Repeat.

***

May 1, 2017

This morning, my CPE supervisor asked me a question that completely stumped me: "Do you ever get silly?" Not, "How do you have a good time?" or "When do you have fun?" but intentional silliness.

After struggling to remember, I answered: "I used to." I felt a sudden and strong yearning for that letting go – safe from labels, judgments, conventionality.

So, naturally, he assigned me the following homework: ask my kids for a lesson in silliness and play and report back what I did next week. Honestly, first homework assignment I've looked forward to in many, many years.

***

July 11, 2017

I often regret opening my mouth to speak a word but never regret closing it to listen for a bit longer.

***

September 23, 2017

We don't need more talking heads; we need more listening hearts.

***

February 7, 2018

My beloved teacher said once that taking a retreat for oneself shouldn't be done with the mindset of taking a break from people. Rather, we should approach the retreat believing that we are giving people a break from ourselves. Profound shift, *subhanAllah*.

***

April 13, 2018

Reflecting on the stories about our beloved Prophet ﷺ told by his wife, Aisha, I'm grateful for and inspired by her example of leadership. If not for her authenticity in sharing about marital life at home and her vulnerability in narrating both her mistakes and achievements as the Prophet's wife, we would not have the wholeness of the Prophet's character today.

***

May 29, 2018

I have been incredibly blessed to study with some of the greatest thinkers and scholars of our time through the Bayan Claremont chaplaincy program. It doesn't escape me that I get to study the Qur'an, *seerah* (prophetic history), *fiqh* (jurisprudence), etc., for my career/degree as well as for my own personal growth. What an honor.

***

July 26, 2018

Several years ago, toward the end of my term on a board, I was given the opportunity to sit with a coach to assess my transition. I remember having worked with this coach in a different capacity where he implied that I was resistant to change. That line stuck in my head and played on a loop until I believed it and even claimed it. It took me many years later to realize that wasn't it at all.

More recently, I was told by a teacher that I rush into decisions hastily, and again, I absorbed that narrative and claimed it. It wasn't until a week ago that I snapped out of it and realized that couldn't be farther from the truth about me.

Moral of the story: watch carefully for narratives or qualities imposed on you by others. Listen for those shaming voices in your head and reflect on whose voice it is and why it's there. And get to know yourself well — it's the first step to loving and embracing yourself, which is a prerequisite to defending your heart, mind, and soul from external forces.

***

February 12, 2019

Feeling sad and frustrated that in this current season of my life I'm moving from one place/task to the next without the luxury of "lingering" in one space for long. My eyes are always on the clock, estimating and calculating when I have to leave to make it to the next thing on time. It's not a really mindful way of living.

The anguish of living life without the ability to linger in spaces ... sigh.

***

September 21, 2019

There's a beautiful Buddhist saying that goes, "Treat others as if they were you, because they are."

Oftentimes, though, I find that compassionate-centered people have no problem treating others with gentleness and tenderness, but when it comes to themselves, they become punitive and self-lacerating.

We talk a lot about embodying kindness and mercy toward others, but we must remember that we, too, deserve self-compassion and a second chance.

Imam Ali (God be pleased with him) is reported to have said, within each one of us is enfolded the entire universe. How wondrous and intricate and beautiful are you! #self-love #revivingthesunnahofcompassion

***

October 17, 2019

I once met with a cancer patient who, shortly after receiving the diagnosis, wondered aloud to me why they got cancer. The patient ate organic-everything, never smoked or drank, exercised, and even abstained from soda, and still, the cancer descended.

Opening up the question, I began to reflect on why we do the "right" thing when we know we cannot control the outcome. If we consider the transactional method, we do certain things in a certain way because we expect a certain outcome, and when the outcome is different than what we expected, we struggle (and rightfully so).

But, if we can adjust our approach to be transformational instead – where we do the "right" thing because it's the right thing to do, with hope for the best but suspending expectation of results – we may be able to move forward free of regret.

Our moral framework is built not around the transactional but around the transformational, that which is best ultimately for our soul and spirit. When we operate out of this moral framework, then, no matter the outcome, we can find comfort that the steps we took to get to the destination are ones that we would do all over again. #surrender #*tasleem* (surrender) #*tawakul* (reliance)

***

October 27, 2019

Two summers ago, I traveled to Germany and Poland with a group of eleven seminarians to study ethics within the context of World War II. We spent two weeks discussing how professionals – lawyers, doctors, journalists, entrepreneurs, and, of course, clergy – could delude themselves into believing that their "small" role did not contribute to the immoral and unethical outcome. They plead ignorance, they minimized their contribution, and some even convinced themselves that they were actually doing the right thing.

The point of that two week trip was to take a really hard look at ourselves as up-and-coming "professionals" and to accept that we can and probably will contribute to unethical and even oppressive behavior in our own spaces.

We don't know what we don't know. I remember again the lessons I learned on that trip — to critically assess for oneself, to avoid group-think, and, above all, to constantly reevaluate our intentions and qualifications for the roles we occupy, because having good and sincere intentions isn't enough.

Who do you oversee in your professional and personal life? Who falls under your care? Are they living to their best potential? Are they equipped to succeed or to fail? And what's your role in that?

It's scary to think that we can be an accomplice to oppression and injustice, even with the best of intentions. God help and forgive us. *Ameen.*

***

November 12, 2019

Waiting for my breakfast order, I watched the employee wrap the sandwich and place it in an open brown paper bag. He called out my name as I approached the counter. Instead of pushing the bag toward me and moving on, he took an extra twenty seconds to line up the folds on the bag ever so perfectly and crease the top over to make a sharp seal. He worked with such precision, such deliberation that I couldn't help but think he was handling a bag of treasure for royalty. When the bag was folded and sealed to his satisfaction, he held it out for me with both hands and a smile. Stunned, I accepted the bag feeling seen and cared for.

Not a single word needed to be exchanged. That's *ihsan* (excellence). That's love and service. #revivingthesunnahofcompassion

***

CHAPTER FOUR

RETURNING

March 19, 2017

This past week began with an elderly patient gasping her last breaths of air as I whispered Qur'an into her ear at the request of her tearful daughters, and ended yesterday with a lifeless newborn brought into the ER.

***

April 20, 2017

I was doing rounds on one of the hospital units when I came across a middle aged woman sitting on the floor, her back propped against the wall. I introduced myself and asked if she was okay. She shared that her father, a patient in the room across from where she was sitting, was actively dying. "I can see the Angel of Death outside his door right now," she said.

I asked if they had a faith tradition, to which she laughed and said, "My dad is an atheist. He's a scientist ... doesn't believe what he cannot prove. But me, I'm spiritual. I mean, just look at a flower. You can't tell me that wasn't made by a Creator."

She saw what many people never see, even though she grew up in a house with no religion, no mention of God.

Truly, God guides whom He wills.

***

August 14, 2017

There's something about bearing witness to somebody's last moments of life at the hospital. It's all about the tenderness between generations of family members paying their respects to a matriarch or patriarch. It's the kissing of the hand, the smoothing of the hair, the fanning of the face, the massaging of the feet, the tucking in of the blanket, the whispered words in the ear.

When God talks about mercy enveloping those who visit the sick, I have to say it's more than palpable. What an honor to be a part of it as a stranger.

***

October 11, 2017

One of my favorite images of chaplaincy is chaplain as "Intimate Stranger."

Today, I was honored to bear witness to patients and staff grappling with cancer diagnoses, recent deaths of parents and children, hopelessness, and letting go of basic function. With all but one of these cases today, it was my first time meeting these people. And yet, they invited me into the most sacred and private moments of their journey.

In one case, from the hallway, I caught an older son leaning over to kiss his father, who lay in the bed dying. I immediately felt embarrassed and humbled for seeing that. Who am I to share in this pain? Thank you, God, for the privilege.

***

May 23, 2018

I learned today from the palliative care team that the younger the cancer patient, the more likely they will "fight" through their prognosis and endure extreme suffering for the sake of their loved ones (i.e. child/ren). In some ways, it's like the patient has to show their loved ones that they did everything they could before succumbing. And even though the care team knows where the train is headed, we have to find a way to support the patient and their family members in this decision to continue treatment and endure incredible suffering because it's not our job to speed up the journey. The patient and their family members have to work through each part of the journey, step by step, just like members of the care team did on their first case.

I digested all this while watching a 40 year old terminal cancer patient hospitalized for massive pain prepare for discharge and another round of chemo.

***

June 3, 2018

In our modern-day culture we have come to believe that an all-loving, all-caring God will offer us a world in which death is optional. When we are not in grief, we can see that is not true, but when life is at its toughest, it's easy to believe that God callously uses death as punishment. The reality is that God gives us a life cycle that includes death. We live in a world of duality. God created day with night, light with shadow, and life with death.

—*On Grief and Grieving*

I read so many Qur'anic reminders in this excerpt. The Qur'an shows a beautiful balance of God's compassion/forgiveness but also that He will test all of us with some form of loss. The Qur'an regularly reminds us that this life is fleeting, that we will die, that the next life is where we invest. And the Qur'an so poetically uses duality to teach these many lessons.

The greatest gift of my chaplaincy job at the hospital is facing death and mortality every day. What I've learned: Serve others, love others, and seek His forgiveness always.

This is Islam.

***

June 11, 2018

So whoever desires to meet his Lord, he should do good deeds and not associate anyone in the worship of his Lord.
—*Qur'an 18:110*

Last week, I met with a 90-something year old woman who decided to put herself on hospice. The night before, she called her children and grandchildren to her hospital room to deliver the news. They wanted her to live, she told me, but she insisted that her decision was final. "I'm ready to meet God," she said, "I don't know when He will take me, but I'm ready."

I wondered about this for myself. Am I ready to meet my Lord? Do I need to live till my 90s to share her confidence, her resolve? If not my 90s, then when? What is that "magical" number that says I've given it my all, I've done all that I can?

***

September 5, 2018

Today, I sat with an elderly patient with a terminal illness who wanted to spend some time reflecting on his life. His main questions to himself were: 1) Did I contribute meaningfully, and 2) Is my belief strong enough and will it remain strong at my time of death.

His tearful and earnest reminiscing touched my heart. How blessed is he to have the time and to make the time for this level of introspection and subsequent adjustment.

***

December 20, 2018

What an honor to be asked to read a patient's favorite two chapters of the Qur'an as he nears his final hours of life on this earth. This patient spent every night in prayer reciting these two chapters, and in his last moments, Allah facilitates for somebody to recite those two chapters for him. Allah is truly Ever Watchful, Most Merciful to His beloveds.

***

March 27, 2019

Several attempts at resuscitation. Family's heartbreaking realization that the end is here. Clinicians' flurry of action settles into an abrupt, eerie stillness. Eyes on the monitor as the soul makes its transition. A family's tearful goodbye. One last pleading to "wake up, please!" Doctor calling time. Chaplain requests a moment of silence.

A body. A shell. Another soul returns to its Maker.

***

August 27, 2019

I was visiting with a cancer patient today who, in the midst of the painful pangs of oncoming death, could only call out for their mother — over and over.

It only now occurred to me that the comfort of a parent's love is the closest thing we have in this terrestrial life to understanding God's love for us.

And perhaps in the hours before our soul wrenches free of our body, we yearn to be reunited and immersed in the safety and cushion of that sacred womb.

***

CHAPTER FIVE

GOD'S PLAN

May 14, 2018

Recently, I received a referral for a patient for a spiritual care visit. In tracking down this referral, I was told that the patient just returned from a procedure and wouldn't be awake for the next several hours. The staff member helping me was perplexed as to why I would be asked to visit a sleeping patient so soon out of surgery. With no clear answer, I touched base with a clinician caring for the patient and explained that I received the referral but would come back later given the circumstances.

The clinician agreed, then hesitated before asking, "Are chaplains only for patients?" I told her that I was there for anybody — patients, families, staff. She looked at me with tears flooding her eyes. "It has just been one of those days," she said, and proceeded to talk. We had a deep conversation and developed a friendship despite me not really knowing her at all before.

Neither of us missed that we met because of a "random" referral that nobody could figure out why or from where it came. God sends us help from unexpected sources. Trust that God will sustain us and is present in difficult times. *#tawakul* #withhardshipcomesease

***

August 27, 2018

When Musa (Moses) and *Bani Israel* (the children of Israel) trekked through the barren, dry desert, Allah offered them the best and most rare of sustenance: *mann* and *salwa* (heavenly foods of manna and quails). But

54

Bani Israel couldn't see past the status quo to appreciate the gift.

When we're trekking through a difficult and dangerous "desert," we watch for Allah's new sustenance for us. No matter the challenge, Allah is with us, sustaining and guiding and nourishing. Sometimes it's just a matter of us letting go of what no longer benefits us and have trust that new people, new locations, new relationships, and new offers will.

***

November 27, 2018

The whole point of challenges in our life is to grow ever closer to Him. Don't let *Shaytan* (Satan) fool you into thinking you're doomed because you're struggling with something. Keep your ship pointed toward Him no matter the intensity of the storm raging around you, threatening to pull you away. Struggle, and keep struggling, and do it all with a deep trust in Allah's Plan and through sincere prayer for His Help. If you fail today, get up tomorrow and try again. Allah will not fail you.

***

January 22, 2019

Consider the story of Maryam's mother, the wife of Imran. In the Qur'an, she prays to God and dedicates her unborn child to His service not knowing that she would be delivering a baby girl. Some of the scholars relate that the practice of dedicating a male child to the total worship of God and service to His sanctified place of ritual was required of previous monotheist communities.

For the mother of Maryam, bearing the child sought the honor and high station of contributing her own offspring to such a dedication. Remarkably, her oath was not only accepted but answered in a way far exceeding her own understanding of how her prayer may be fulfilled. The daughter she gave birth to was far better than any son she had hoped for and requested. I learned from my teacher that a typical son would have been a common religious functionary of his times, one of no doubt many male youth dedicated to service of the Sacred House. However, this particular daughter was granted a station like no other woman, including giving miraculous birth to the penultimate Prophet. Moreover, she would not give birth to more than one child, but that one was a means for the greatest possible blessing.

In either case, Maryam's mother would have been blessed by the offspring granted to her and pleased with God's will, but the full consequence of her intent and desire to please God could not have been known to her, nor even witnessed by her own eye. She merely lifted her heart to the Lord of the Worlds, sought to make her life and very offspring dedicated wholly to God, and by His Mercy, was given the best of answers and outcomes.

This story resonates with my understanding of trusting in the Goodness of God and His Plan. Like Maryam's mother, I make plans and prayers without knowing what the future holds while God, in His Infinite Wisdom, knows the minutiae of my life and facilitates my affairs such that not only are my plans and prayers fulfilled, they are fulfilled in the best and sometimes unexpected ways.

***

April 24, 2019

I recently visited with a patient whose cancer had disabled his speech. With only a pad of paper, pen, and hand gestures, he struggled to "talk" and I struggled to understand how he has been holding on in the face of imminent death. Several minutes in, amid much frustration from both ends, I finally interpreted what he so adamantly wanted me to hear: "Is God in your life?"

The question touched something deep and powerful in me that tears immediately sprang to my eyes. I saw the tears mirrored in his own. "Yes," I whispered. He nodded and patted his heart, saying, "me, too." Our eyes locked as our souls filled in the gaps.

Suddenly, I understood everything.

***

September 26, 2019

As I stepped out of the hospital for a brief respite, I found a gentleman clutching his phone and a hospital pamphlet looking very confused. In asking him if he needed help, I learned that he was searching for his car location, which was saved on his phone. I told him I was happy to help him in his search.

We ended up walking around the hospital grounds for thirty minutes deeply engrossed in reflections on God, faith, and humanity. "We're all following a map like this one," he said, shaking his phone, "and we all hope to reach our destination." We agreed it was about the journey and the discoveries on that journey, as we were walking it, that mattered.

He didn't subscribe to any particular faith tradition nor did he grow up following one, but he had the most profound insights into the Presence and Majesty of God. "How did you learn this?" I asked him. "I just talk to Him all the time," was his reply, "and when I gather with my family and friends and feel their love for me, for all my flaws and inconsistencies, that's God right there."

Teachers are everywhere and come in all shapes and sizes. Every meeting is a Divine meeting, and God is Ever Present between hearts.

***

November 25, 2019

He who inspired Maryam to eat fruit from the palm in the midst of birthing pangs; He who sent Haroon (Aaron) to support Musa in confronting Pharaoh; He who grew a gourd plant to shade Yunus (Jonah) from the elements; He who made the fire cool for Ibrahim (Abraham) ...

We experience suffering, seemingly insurmountable challenges, discomfort, and hardship. And we learn to look for the resources – human and otherwise – He sends our way, because He, in His Mercy and Generosity, does not set us up to fail.

***

CHAPTER SIX

THE QUR'AN

March 12, 2017

After being tasked by God to visit Pharaoh, Musa prayed:

> Give me a helper from my family, my
> brother Aaron – augment my strength
> through him. Let him share my task so

> that we can glorify You much and
> remember You often: You are always
> watching over us.
> —*Qur'an 20:29-35*

Musa felt overwhelmed with the monstrous task of confronting Pharaoh, so he asked God to strengthen him with a partner.

Interestingly, Musa justified this request by pointing out that a partner will help him to glorify and remember God, implying that community not only provides emotional support but also spiritual support. #chaplaincy

***

June 15, 2017

I think I have a better understanding of the story of Adam and Eve's journey in the Qur'an. When they disobeyed God, a trust was broken and they were suddenly made aware of their exposed bodies. I now understand the sudden awareness. Similarly, things happen between us and people in our lives, and a trust is broken. We can't go back to the pure, innocent relationship. We can't unsee, unfeel, unhear, and unspeak. Something has forever changed, and we gain a new awareness of ourselves that may leave us feeling exposed. We enter into a different reality.

To take this reflection further, I suppose the next step is to follow Adam's example in asking for forgiveness from God and doing what we can to live better in our new reality post-awareness.

***

April 10, 2018

I heard a quote from Jay-Z that made me appreciate the Qur'an on a different level:

> It's what the prophets are since the beginning of time — just poets and musicians. They would tell tales through song. And because they wasn't preaching to you, you let down your guard a bit. You liked the melody. You relaxed. Then you got fed.

Obviously, the parallel isn't exact, but it was enough to help me understand my own fascination with the Qur'an and how its recitation nourishes me in a way that nothing has or will. And on a lesser level, how some songs reach the heart like nothing else can reach.

***

July 15, 2018

I never realized how intertwined women's bodies are with the passing of time. As women track monthly cycles and pregnancy trimesters, they become so aware of the passing days, weeks, and months. Women's bodies – unlike men's – undergo regular seasons of change and renewal, imitating the natural cycles around us. Reminds me of the verse:

> They ask you, [O Muhammad], about the new moons. Say, "They are measurements of time for the people and for Hajj."
> —*Qur'an 2:187*

***

June 8, 2019

In the Qur'an, God describes Himself as "*Nurun 'ala nur*," or Light upon Light (24:35). When I reflect on this beautiful way of capturing God's essence, I'm struck by how the brilliance of light, when shined into a crevice, reaches all surfaces from the shallow to the deepest and darkest of voids.

For those seeking God, remember that He is not only a Constant Presence as you move about your day,

His light bathes and caresses the deepest parts of you, physically and metaphysically. Don't turn outward to find Him; seek Him in your being and in the deep, dark places of your soul. He is there.

***

CHAPTER SEVEN

PRAYER AND

WORSHIP

May 26, 2016

Take a few minutes to pray for somebody by name.
Open your heart and let God plant a name there. You

never know how much that person might need that extra boost today.

***

May 3, 2017

I was taught a lesson in gratitude today at the hospital after praying with a homeless paraplegic patient in his 20s who has lived through abuse, incredible loss, and abandonment. He spent more than half of his prayer aloud with me in sincere thanks to God.

***

March 13, 2018

I realized that, between Muslims, prayers are woven into the tapestry of a conversation. It becomes a fluid exchange of a prayer for you, a prayer for me: "I have so much pain;" "May God grant you peace;" "And grant you peace." Muslims weave prayer into at least five gaps of the day, so eventually, the lines between prayer time and living time are blurred, transforming the mundane into the spiritual. Prayers are fed to the individual constantly, like sustenance fed through an IV line, instead of a one-time gulp of pills from a paper cup.

***

March 16, 2018

My biggest takeaway from the movie, "Bilal" was that all of us are a slave to something and that true freedom is being able to own your desires without the desires owning you.

Putting two and two together, I realized that our tradition methodically trains us to reach this true freedom. We fast for a month to detach from our primal needs; we pray on a schedule to detach from whatever we deem "more important" at that moment; we perform pilgrimage to detach from our daily comforts and even from loved ones (leaving them behind to make the journey); we pay a wealth tax to detach from a proclivity to hoard our wealth for ourselves; and on and on. At every moment of our life here on earth, we are training at a different intensity level. Some of these rituals happen daily, but at a lower intensity. Some of these rituals happen once a year, but at a higher intensity. And some rituals happen once in a lifetime, but are at the highest intensity. We build and build and build.

It's all beautifully orchestrated to the smallest detail.

***

March 27, 2018

I see the five love languages in our five pillars/rituals:

1) Words of affirmation – *shahada* (declaration of faith)
2) Quality time – *salah* (prayer)
3) Physical touch – *sawm* (fasting) (we physically, tangibly feel the worship spiritually and corporally)
4) Gifts – *zakah* (almsgiving)
5) Acts of service – *Hajj* (pilgrimage)

Just as we are each predisposed to a love language, we also find that one pillar nourishes us in different phases and situations of our life. God provides us with such a plentiful toolbox to best connect with Him. Which pillar/ritual/love language resonates with you at this time?

***

October 16, 2018

Recently, I was with a couple of peers (not Muslim) from my age group who were comparing new mindfulness apps to help them manage their stress. One feature caught my attention; one of the apps audibly reminds a person to pause three times a day for a few minutes of breathing and centering.

"Which app do you use?" they asked me. I smiled, thinking about *salah*. "My app calls me to pause five times a day," I replied.

It made me wonder if it may be more effective to "rebrand" *salah* as mindfulness breaks and *adhan* (call to prayer) apps as mindfulness reminders. Would its worth change in the eyes of some?

***

October 26, 2018

I have spent the past two months agonizing over a small work assignment. I devoted close to a dozen hours reflecting, writing, and brainstorming on all different angles of the assignment but ultimately felt stuck. Today, on the morning of the due date with still no breakthrough, I decided to wake up early and utilize the blessings of the *Fajr* (predawn) prayer hours. In ten minutes, my heart and mind aligned, and I had an entire framework written on a topic that I had never considered before but worked perfectly for the assignment.

Lesson for me: Do not underestimate the guidance and wisdoms set forth in our Islamic tradition. Trust and invest in the process; it really does work! *Duaa's* (prayers) appreciated nonetheless.

***

November 30, 2018

If fasting doesn't help us develop will power and delayed self-gratification, we're doing it wrong.

If pilgrimage doesn't help us detach from our daily comforts and self, we're doing it wrong.

If prayer doesn't help us trust in Allah and His Control over matters, we're doing it wrong.

If almsgiving doesn't help us realize that our human race is interdependent and that we will sink without each other, we're doing it wrong.

Religious ritual was prescribed to strengthen our spirituality, not replace it.

***

May 1, 2019

I'm really digging the approach of combining the vertical connection with the horizontal. This year, I'm forgoing the workbooks and checklists and accounting-heavy approach to my Ramadan worship (and for my kids). Rather, I hope to spend more time serving and loving His creation while spending quiet time alone reflecting on Him and listening for Him. My prayer will be, *Ya Allah*, make Yourself known to me and my loved ones. *Ameen.*

***

June 6, 2019

O God!
Publicly I call you
"My Lord"

But in solitude
I call you
"My Beloved"
—Abu Nu'aym Isfahani

When we undergo life's most crushing challenges, when we lose people or precious things or once comforting truths, when we find ourselves grasping for answers that never come, what do we crave more than anything? A friend who can listen fully, give us presence, and make us feel heard and loved. Sometimes we seek advice from this friend, but more often than not, we just

73

so desperately want to be seen and heard and validated in our pain.

Sufi mystics referred to God as *"Doost,"* or Friend because they approached God as such. Their prayers were unfiltered, candid conversations with God wherein they felt the freedom and comfort to vent, question, cry, and break apart. Until I found myself in the midst of pain and loss, my *duaa* was largely scripted, memorized, and formulaic, though not insincere but admittedly detached. God became my *Doost* on lone car rides as tears streamed down my face, masked by large sunglasses. He became my Beloved when I pleaded for relief and mercy. He became Real when I found myself humbled and unable to verbalize my challenges to any other human because nobody but God could truly understand.

Then it dawned on me, prayer is like that conversation with your friend: We speak to God not always seeking advice but merely looking for a Comforting Presence, a Listening Ear, a Validating Source, knowledge that Somebody is Witness to our unbearable pain — at 2 in the morning, at 6 in the evening, and all seconds in between. Remove whatever shackles stand between you and your *Doost*. Try calling on your Beloved today rather than your Lord.

***

June 14, 2019

A new appreciation I gained this morning about *salah*: incorporating ritual worship five times a day – often at times deemed "inconvenient" for those of us living the Rat Race – not only teaches us about our utter dependence on God, it also gently forces us out of a "vending machine" approach to conversing with God. In other words, *salah* teaches us that we don't approach God only when we want to request something from Him. Our relationship with Him can be so much more than that.

Transformational, not transactional, ritual.

***

CHAPTER EIGHT

CHILDREN

September 21, 2016

My son is handwriting a letter to Steph Curry to invite him for dinner at our house. Here were his sincere questions to me: "Is it okay that I told him dinner? I'll help cook, don't worry;" "Mom, do you mind if his bodyguards have to come, too?;" "Isn't it a good time to invite him now since the NBA season hasn't started?"

I'm jealous of his and his sister's profound optimism.

***

November 23, 2016

Due to Thanksgiving break, the kids spent a couple of hours with me at work at the hospital this morning. Walking to my office, my son witnessed a grieving family in the waiting room. Their loved one was taking her last breaths at 90 years old. When we entered the office, my son began to cry. Alarmed, I held him in my arms while he asked me, "why does she have to die?" We talked about death and mortality in the Qur'an and what that means for our time here on earth. It was a sobering but necessary conversation.

On our way out of the office, he saw some of the family members near the elevators and wordlessly went up to them and gave them each a big hug. My heart is so full.

***

November 8, 2017

Yesterday, my son came home from school frustrated and in a bad mood. He said he had a bad day but didn't want to discuss further. We got home, where he proceeded to whine and pout about every little thing and then fell asleep on the couch.

After an hour and a half, I woke him up, and he was still grouchy. He had school homework, Qur'an class, and basketball practice. I looked at him and saw the exhaustion in his face, and I remembered myself feeling that way a few weeks ago. During that time, a supervisor gave me permission to leave work to go home and self-care, which I did. It took someone older and more senior in position to teach me how to give myself permission and let go of "should" and just be.

Having experienced the freedom of that afternoon, I told my son that we could skip all his commitments for that day and just be together. We ended up going out for ice cream instead. We self-cared. I'm grateful to those who knew me well enough to extend that permission, and I'm grateful that I can pass down that permission to a kid who experiences scheduling/ commitments a lot like I do.

***

December 6, 2017

My son made me laugh today when he said, "When I make a *duaa*, I imagine '*ameen*' as the 'Send' button."

***

February 22, 2018

My son loves hip hop. I do not.

He loves basketball. I'm indifferent about it.

He follows sports news. I do not.

He wants to grow his hair long. I'm not thrilled.

He thinks athletes and rap stars are the coolest. I do not.

One thing we do have in common: we're introverted and prefer not to talk a lot. Combining all this information, I realized yesterday that if I want any chance at having a conversation and a connection with my son, I need to be more open minded about his interests and passion instead of expecting him to be just like me.

I asked him to show me that music video by Drake he was trying to tell me about the other day when I had just rolled my eyes in response. He got so excited, he plopped down on the couch and patted the seat next to him saying, "Mama! Sit here!" We watched "God's Plan" together and talked about why he liked it. While the sound of Drake's voice made me think of nails on a chalkboard, I was really happy to see him so happy to share something important (to him) with me. These kids continue to teach me and push my limits, and I am grateful.

***

September 10, 2018

We as a community must elevate the level of conversation addressing issues of beauty standards, body image, self-love, and self-esteem for our girls (and boys, actually).

My 10-year old daughter told me, tearfully: "Mama, I don't think all that 'love yourself no matter what' stuff everybody always says is working."

The words are being heard but are still missing the target. Allah help us.

***

December 15, 2018

Yesterday, my kids' school hosted the grandparents of middle school students for "Grandparents Day." This year, students were assigned the task of interviewing their grandparent(s) to collect stories about their childhood, milestones, and immigration journey. The project is called, "Preserving Our Legacy," with the aim of honoring, archiving, and claiming the American Muslim history and narrative.

I cannot describe the feelings that surfaced when my son sat across from my mother and father in a small conference room, his laptop recording as he listened to their stories, exchanged memories, and saw for the first time his *Anna* (grandma) and *Jiddo* (grandpa) as children and teenagers in old photos. The same feelings emerged when noting the pride and love in my parents' faces as they relayed their precious life story to their almost-teenage grandson.

I am grateful to the school for providing this space and opportunity for my son to connect with my parents in a meaningful, powerful way and for giving him the opportunity to dutifully preserve and carry their precious legacy. Allah protect them all. *Ameen.*

***

May 15, 2019

This Ramadan, I find myself getting emotional thinking about and reflecting on the gift of family meals twice a day — *suhur* (predawn meal) and *iftar* (breaking fast). In our family, our hectic schedules rarely afford an opportunity for a single joint meal around the table, and for one month out of the year, we are given the blessing of two joint meals daily.

I've already learned much about my kids' table habits in the last ten days, and I love our storytelling and laughter sharing. Ramadan is such a gift, with so many layers that keeps revealing itself to me as I grow older. *Alhamdulillah* (praise God).

***

December 21, 2019

I was sitting on the ground, my daughter up on the couch, when she asked me, "If Prophet Muhammad was here with us right now, what would you do?" I thought about it carefully and replied, "I'd ask him if I was doing the right thing, as he taught it. How about you?" Without hesitation, she said, "I'd give him a hug."

I became awash with envy at her response and then with immense sadness at my next thought: "Would the Prophet accept a hug from me, an adult woman?"

You see, I operate from *shariah* (rules for Muslim life) while my daughter operates from *baseerah* (inner heart's sight).

***

ABOUT THE AUTHOR

Chaplain Sondos Kholaki serves as a hospital staff chaplain and a community chaplain in Southern California. She is board-certified with the Association of Professional Chaplains (APC). Sondos earned a Master of Divinity degree in Islamic Chaplaincy from Bayan Islamic Graduate School / Claremont School of Theology as the recipient of the Fathi Osman Academic Excellence award and a Bachelor of Arts in English and Creative Writing from UCLA as a Regents Scholar. Sondos completed five units of Clinical Pastoral Education (CPE) residency where she served care seekers of all faiths and educated staff and volunteers on Muslim spiritual care. Sondos is the co-editor of *Mantle of Mercy: Islamic Chaplaincy in North America* (fall 2021). She also serves as Vice President of Healthcare for the Association of Muslim Chaplains (AMC). Sondos enjoys sipping a perfectly brewed cup of coffee, listening to Quran recitation by Turkish reciters, and singing her heart out at spiritual gatherings. She is married and has two children.

Made in the USA
Middletown, DE
27 April 2021

38228222R00066